Science Sight

Polar Regions

by Sally St. John

ISBN 978-0-545-24809-9

Photographs © 2010: cover: Minden Pictures/Matthias Breiter; back cover top: iStockphoto/Jan Will; back cover bottom: iStockphoto/Dmitry Deshevykh; page 1: ShutterStock, Inc./Vladimir Melnik; page 2 inset: ShutterStock, Inc./AridOcean; pages 2 background, 3: Getty Images/Joseph Van Os; page 4: ShutterStock, Inc./Nik Niklz; page 5 main: Getty Images/Sue Flood; page 5 inset: iStockphoto/Alexandre Moroz; page 6: iStockphoto/Dmitry Deshevykh; page 7 main: Alamy Images/blickwinkel; page 7 inset: Getty Images/Pater Lilja; page 8: Photo Researchers, NY/Ed Cesar; page 9: ShutterStock, Inc./Daniel Hebert; page 10: iStockphoto/Mogens Trolle; page 11 main: Seapics.com/Phillip Colla; page 11 inset: iStockphoto/Bruno Monteny; page 12 main: iStockphoto/Jan Will; page 12 inset: ShutterStock, Inc./Armin Rose; page 13: iStockphoto/Keith Szafranski; page 14: iStockphoto/thp73; page 15: iStockphoto/Michael Ofiachra; page 16: ShutterStock, Inc./AridOcean.

Photo research by Veroniqua Quinteros; Design by Holly Grundon

12 11 10 9 8 7 6 5 13 14 15/0

Printed in the U.S.A. 40

First printing, November 2010

SCHOLASTIC INC.

NEW YORK • TORONTO • LONDON • AUCKLAND
SYDNEY • MEXICO CITY • NEW DELHI • HONG KONG

Polar Regions

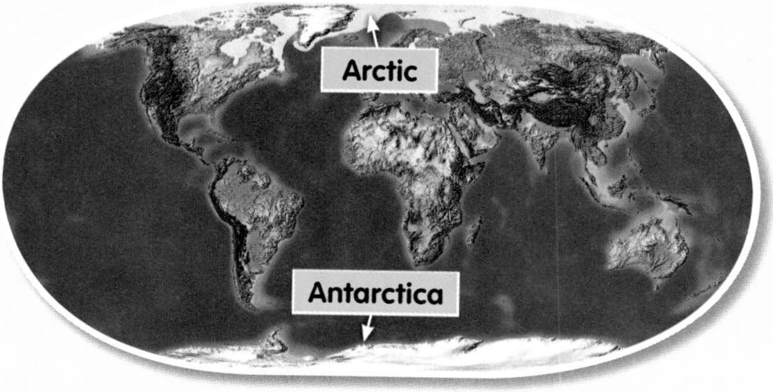

The Arctic is at the top of the world. Antarctica is at the bottom of the world. These two very **cold** places are called the polar regions.

Welcome to the polar regions!

Fast Fact

The polar regions are covered with ice and snow. Temperatures can reach -100°F or lower.

This **cold, white** habitat is just **right for** many animals.

polar bear
Fast Fact
Polar bears
live in the Arctic.
Their favorite
food is seals.

This **cold, white** habitat is just **right for** polar bears!

walrus

Fast Fact

Walruses live in the Arctic.
Some weigh as much as a car!

This **cold, white** habitat is just **right for** walruses!

arctic fox

Fast Fact

These foxes live in the Arctic. Their thick fur helps keep them warm.

This **cold, white** habitat is just **right for** arctic foxes!

reindeer

Fast Fact

Reindeer live in the Arctic. They travel in herds.

This **cold**, **white** habitat is just **right for** reindeer!

ermine
Fast Fact
Ermines live in the Arctic. They are a kind of weasel.

This **cold, white** habitat is just **right for** ermines!

Fast Fact

Snowy owls live in the Arctic. They have great eyesight and hearing.

This **cold, white** habitat is just **right for** snowy owls!

Fast Fact

Leopard seals live in Antarctica. A layer of fat called "blubber" helps them survive the cold.

This **cold, white** habitat is just **right for** leopard seals!

Fast Fact

Blue whales migrate to Antarctica in the summer. One whale weighs as much as 30 elephants!

This **cold, white** habitat is just **right for** blue whales!

emperor penguin

Fast Fact

Emperor penguins live in Antarctica. They can slide on their bellies.

This **cold**, **white** habitat is just **right for** emperor penguins . . .

emperor penguin chick

. . . and their babies, too!

Sight Word Review

Point to each sight word. Then read it aloud.

Sight Word Fill-ins

Use one sight word from the box to finish each sentence.

cold	**for**
right	**white**

1. The temperature gets very ______ in the polar regions.

2. Penguins are black and ______.

3. People who think polar bears live in the Arctic are ______.

4. Arctic foxes grow thick fur ______ warmth.

ANSWERS: 1. cold 2. white 3. right 4. for

All About Polar Regions

Ask a grown-up to read this with you.

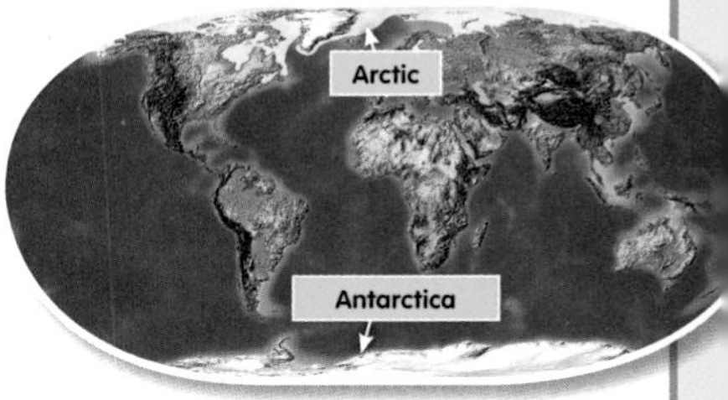

The polar regions include two parts of the Earth—the very top and the very bottom. Both places are super cold. The top of the Earth is called the Arctic and the bottom is called Antarctica.

Parts of many countries, such as Finland, Canada, and Russia, are in the Arctic. Animals that make their home in this harsh environment must adapt to the extreme conditions to survive. The fur of some Arctic animals, such as foxes, turns white during the long winter. This makes it hard for predators to see them. Other animals, such as reindeer, migrate long distances in search of food.

The Arctic may be cold, but Antarctica is colder. Antarctica is the chilliest continent. The coldest temperature ever recorded on Earth (-129°F) was recorded in Antarctica. But even here, animals can be found. In fact, many penguins and seals live in the frigid ocean off the coast of Antarctica. It is also home to blue whales, the largest animals on the planet. Blue whales feed on some of the world's smallest creatures—microscopic plankton.